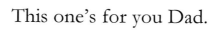

This one's for you Dad.

Triangle Loom Weaving

Twills 'N More

Volume 2

By Patricia Herman

www.lulu.com

www.lulu.com

Text by Patricia Herman © 2010
Photography by Patricia Herman © 2010

ISBN 978-0-557-62824-7

Table of Contents

Crossroads

1. Left: *O1-U1*
2. Right: U1 then, *O3-U2-O1-U2*
3. Left: O2 then, *U1-O1-U1-O2-U1-O2*
4. Right: O1 then, U1-O2-U1-O2-U1-O1*
5. Left: O1 then, U1-O2-U1-O1-U1-O2*
6. Right: O1-U1-O1 then, *U2-O3-U2-O1*
7. Left: *O1-U1*
8. Right: *O1-U1*

Tips:
Middle nail to center design is Step 4 or use Step 1
* = Repeat O = Over warp thread U= Under warp thread Plain weave at top

Adapted from <u>Patterns for the Weavette</u> by Licia Conforti

Shrug
[One size fits most]

Materials:
Loom used- rectangle 32" X 18"
Yarn- Color A, 360 yards
Yarn- Color B, 240 yards

Directions:
Weave 2 matching rectangles OR weave
eight 2 foot triangles and join them to form
a rectangle.

To create the arms of the shrug, measure
20" from the end of rectangle towards the
center of the garment.

Whipstitch the seam on both the left and
right sides.

Finish the edges of the garment by
crocheting a decorative edge around
the cuffs and body of the shrug.

Crocheted edge shown here is a Picot stitch.

Color changes were made every 17th nail for this project.

Model Klohie Kuehne

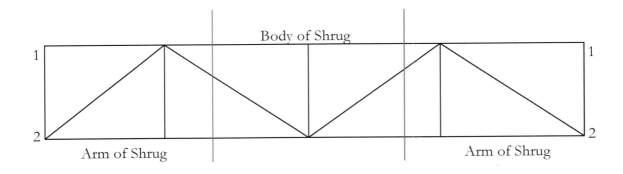

Arms of Shrug- fold #1 to meet #2, measure 20" from end towards middle of fabric and
whipstitch the arm seam.

Arrows

1. Left: *O3-U1-O1-U3-O1-U1-O1-U1*
2. Right: U2 then, *O3-U2-O1-U2-O1-U3*
3. Left: *O3-U2-O3-U1-O2-U1*
4. Right: *O1-U3-O3-U2-O1-U2*
5. Left: *O1-U1-O1-U1-O3-U1-O1-U3*
6. Right: U2 then, O1-U1-O1-U3*
7. Left: *O3-U1-O1-U3-O1-U1-O1-U1*
8. Right: U2 then, *O3-U2-O1-U2-O1-U3*
9. Left: *O3-U2-O3-U1-O2-U1*
10. Right: *O1-U3-O3-U2-O1-U2*
11. Left: *O1-U1-O1-U1-O3-U1-O1-U3*
12. Right: U2 then, *O1-U1-O1-U3*

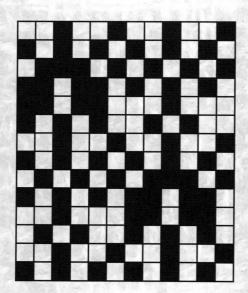

Tips:

Middle nail is Step 5 and cut a tail long enough to weave Step 6 to the top rail.

* = Repeat
O = Over warp thread
U= Under warp thread

Plain weave at top

© Designed by Patricia Herman- 2009

Crop top
[Size Small to Medium]

Model Klohie Kuehne

Materials:
Loom used- 18 inch square
Yarn- Color A, 150 yards
Yarn- Color B, 150 yards
Yarn- Novelty for neck trim, 20 yards

Directions:

Weave two 18" squares OR four 2 foot triangles which are joined together to form 2 squares.

Laying both squares on top of each other, Stitch both shoulder seams, leaving a neck opening of 11".

Stitch both side seams, leaving 9" open for the arm holes. Crochet a decorative edge around bottom of the crop top and the arm holes.
The stitch used in the picture a double crochet stitch.
The neck opening is trimmed with a handspun "Icicle Yarn", but any novelty yarn can be used OR finish with a crocheted edge of choice.

Color changes for the Crop Top were done every 13th nail for this project.

[Front and back the same]

Neck opening

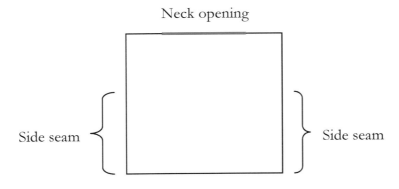

Side seam   Side seam

Ribbing

1. Left: *O3-U1*
2. Right: *O1-U3*
3. Left: O1 then, *U1-O3*
4. Right: U2 then *O1-U3*

<table>
<tr><td>Tips:</td></tr>
<tr><td>Middle nail is Step #1</td></tr>
<tr><td>* = Repeat
O = Over warp thread
U = Under warp thread

Plain weave at top</td></tr>
</table>

Adapted from <u>Patterns for the Weavette</u> by Licia Conforti

Mittens

[Size fits Adult Medium to Large]

Materials:

Loom used- 9 inch square AND 4 inch square
Yarn- Color A, 60 yards
Yarn- Color B, 60 yards
Size 5- Double point knitting needles
    OR 9 inch Cable needles

Directions:

Weave two matching 9 inch squares for
the body of the mitten and two matching
4 inch squares for the thumbs.

Model Rose Ann Kuehne

Fold the 9 inch square in half. Measure the
hand from the tip of the longest finger
down to the top of the thumb fold. [This is where the thumb will be stitched to the body
of the mitten.] Seam the body of the mitten from the thumb fold up to the fingertips.

With a doubled strand of yarn and the tapestry needle, run the yarn in a gathering stitch at
the top of the mitten. Gather the fabric to close the opening and knot the yarn to hold the
gathering in place.

Form the thumb by folding the 4 inch square in half and seam the edges together. Gather
the top of the thumb as with the mitten, and turn the thumb right side out.

Place the thumb right side to right side of the mitten, [the thumb will be inside the mitten,
with the opening for the thumb flush to the mitten.] Seam the edge of the thumb opening
completely around to the body of the mitten. Seam the remaining side seams of the body
of the mitten together under the thumb opening. It varies from 2 to 4 or more stitches
depending on the size of your hand.

Turn the mitten right side out. Using your knitting needles, pick up the loops of the woven
mitten and knit a 3 inch ribbed cuff for the mitten.

Color changes were done using every 8th nail for this project.

Fold here   Gather   Right side out

Side seam

Position of thumb to sew to mitten body

Knit ribbed cuff ....^

Wacky Waffle Weave

Plain weave until there are four warp threads on the loom then........

1. Left: *O2-U2*
2. Right: *U2-O1*
3. Left: *U1-O2*
4. Right: *O1-U1*

Tips:
Middle nail is Step #3 and cut a tail long enough to weave Step #4 to the top rail.
* = Repeat O = Over warp thread U = Under warp thread Plain weave at top

© Designed by Patricia Herman- 2009

Hooded Scarf

[One size fits all.]

Materials:

Loom used- 2 foot triangle
Yarn- Variegated yarn, 350 yards

Directions:

Weave five 2 foot triangles and join to form a long scarf.

Fold scarf in half and seam 12 inches down from fold.

Single crochet the long sides of the scarf and place fringe on both ends.

Model Klohie Kuehne

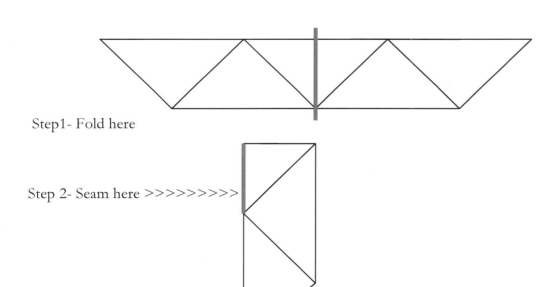

Step1- Fold here

Step 2- Seam here >>>>>>>>>

Hugs & Kisses

1. Left: *O3-U2-O1-U3-O1-U2*
2. Right: *O2-U1*
3. Left: *O2-U3-O2-U1-O3-U1*
4. Right: O1 then, *U1-O2*
5. Left: U1 then, *O1-U2-O3-U2-O1-U3*
6. Right: *O1-U1*

Tips:

Middle nail is Step #5, cut a tail long enough to weave Step # 6 up to the top rail.

* = Repeat
O = Over warp thread
U = Under warp thread

Plain weave at top

*Please note that there is a float over 5 weft threads, this is normal for this weave structure.

Childs Hat

[Fits Pre-school to First Grade]

Materials:

Loom used- 9 inch Diamond Loom
Yarn used- Color A, 40 yards
Yarn used- Color B, 40 yards

Directions:

Weave two 9 inch Diamonds.

Lay the diamonds on top of one another.

Crochet a decorative edge along the peak of the hat. This hat has a Picot edge crocheted on it. The edge will remain exposed- so make it FUN.

Model Kameron Kuehne

Open up hat and crochet an edge along the front and back. The picture features a Single crochet stitch along the base of the hat.

Add braided ties to each end of the hat by taking 3 long stands of yarn which are folded in half. Pull the loop end through the crochet edge in the corner of the hat. Then pull the strands of yarn through the loop and snug the loop up to the hat. Braid the strands and finish with a knot at the end of the braid.

Color changes were done every 14th nail for this project.

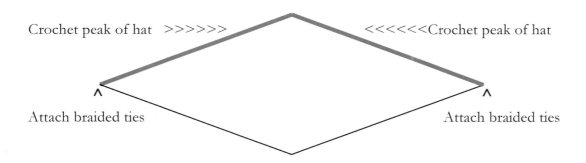

Crochet peak of hat >>>>>>   <<<<<<Crochet peak of hat

Attach braided ties   Attach braided ties

2/2 Twill

1. Left: * O2-U2*
2. Right: *O2-U2*

Tips:
Middle nail is Step #1, cut a tail long enough to weave Step # 2 up to the top rail.
* = Repeat O = Over warp thread U = Under warp thread Plain weave at top

Zig Zag Scarf

[One size fits all]

Materials:

Loom used- 5 inch Triangle
Yarn used- 100 yards

Directions:

Weave fifteen 5 inch Triangles.

Lay eight Triangles out, tip touching tip, in a straight line
with the point facing towards you.

Position the remaining seven Triangles with the point
facing away from you along the hypotenuse
AND the end tip of the first triangle will be shifted
to the halfway mark on the bottom triangle.

Model Klohie Kuehne

Whipstitch the triangles together. When adding a triangle at the end tip, place one end loop
over the new end loop to help maintain the correct spacing along the scarf.

Crochet a decorative edge all around the joined triangle to finish the scarf. Yep- you
guessed it; I used a Picot crochet stitch as the edging.

Whipstitch to join triangles

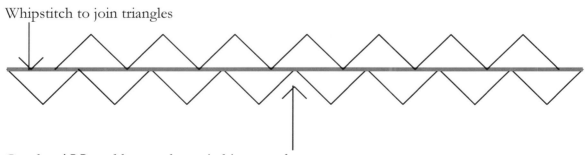

Overlap **ALL** end loops when stitching together

Steps & Ladder

1. Left: *U3-O1-U1-O1*
2. Right: *U1-O3-U1-O1*
3. Left: U1-O1 then, *U3-O1-U1-O1*
4. Right: U1 then, *O1- U1-O1-U3*
5. Left: *U1-O1-U1-O3*
6. Right: *O2-U1-O1-U2*

Tips:

Middle nail is Step #1

* = Repeat
O = Over warp thread
U = Under warp thread

Plain weave at top

Adapted from Patterns for the Weavette by Licia Conforti

Felted Slippers

Materials:

Loom used- square
4" size Infant use worsted wt yarn
9" size Toddler use worsted wt yarn
12" size Small use worsted wt yarn
18" size Medium using sport wt yarn
    size Large using bulky wt yarn
Yarn- should be 100% wool or blends
of wool and natural animal fibers.
DO NOT use superwash wool
as it will not felt.

Leather lacing or ribbon

Directions:

Weave two squares in desired size.

For each slipper-

Fold square in half. Using a single crochet stitch, close one short side to form the heel/back of the slipper.

Using a double length of yarn and a tapestry needle, gather the other short side to begin forming the toe box. Pull the stitches together and secure the gathered fabric with a knot.

Measure approx 1/3 of the length of the slipper, and whipstitch from the gathered toe to 1/3 of the length of the slipper to complete the toe box. Turn fabric right side out.

Crochet an edge around the opening of the slipper. Place the slippers in a top loading washing machine with a few lint free bath towels and laundry soap. Wash the slippers for a full Hot/Cold cycle. When desired size, block and lay out to dry.

Finish by taking a strand of leather laces or ribbon and sew in long stitches around the top of the opening. This helps to keep the shape of the slipper and adjust the fit for comfort.

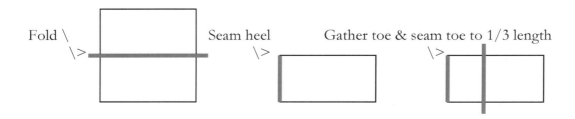

Fold \\ \\>   Seam heel \\>   Gather toe & seam toe to 1/3 length \\>

CPSIA information can be obtained
at www.ICGtesting.com
Printed in the USA
LVRC02n0837230817
546046LV00005B/8